Who Were the Navajo Code Talkers?

by James Buckley Jr.

illustrated by Gregory Copeland

Penguin Workshop

For everyone who gives their time and talents
to help keep people free—JB

To a man of exceptional character, Jerry—GC

PENGUIN WORKSHOP
An imprint of Penguin Random House LLC, New York

First published in the United States of America by Penguin Workshop,
an imprint of Penguin Random House LLC, New York, 2021

Visit us online at penguinrandomhouse.com.

Library of Congress Control Number: 2021020923

Printed in the United States of America

ISBN 9780399542657 (paperback)   10 9 8 7 6 5
ISBN 9780399542664 (library binding)   10 9 8 7 6 5 4 3 2 1

Contents

Who Were the Navajo Code Talkers?

As loud explosions echoed off the rocky island, Samuel Holiday leaped off the landing craft as the huge metal machine slammed into the beach. Samuel was a United States Marine. And the beach was on Iwo Jima, an island in the Pacific Ocean that was held by the Japanese as they battled the United States in World War II. Bullets pinged all around Samuel, while bombs sent huge plumes of black sand into the air. Samuel did his best to walk toward a safe position, but the sand was loose and shifted constantly. Every step was a huge struggle. As he plunged ahead, he saw Marines who had been killed almost as soon as they stepped ashore, lying where they fell.

Samuel clutched his rifle and shouldered the big radio on his back. He had to make it through safely. He had an important job to do. Samuel was one of the Navajo code talkers. These specially trained Marines made sure that thousands of US soldiers, sailors, ships, and planes could get their messages through safely without the Japanese being able to read them. Using their Diné language, the code talkers had become a vital part of the US Marines' mission. Without a secure way to communicate, that mission on Iwo Jima might end in disaster.

Samuel dug out a place where he was safe from bullets for the moment. He and his partner, Dan Akee, set up their radio gear.

"Bil-dah-has-tanh-ya," Samuel said over the radio. *"Al-tah-je-jay yoehi ashdla!"* On the other end of the call, another Navajo code talker was listening. He told his own partner what Samuel had said: "Pinned down! Attack Sector Five!" The order was passed to Marine artillery. Moments later, bombs landed in front of Samuel,

destroying the secret position of the enemy soldiers. The Japanese radio operators who were also listening had no idea what Samuel had said, and their location had been exposed.

Samuel and the other code talkers were in constant danger on Iwo Jima. "The [gun]fire was so intense, men were being killed all around me, and we were pinned down and couldn't move," remembered code talker Teddy Draper. "I kept wondering if I was going to live through the day or be killed in my foxhole." (A foxhole is a dugout pit big enough to hold one or two soldiers.)

Teddy and Samuel did live, and thanks to more than four hundred Navajo code talkers, so did thousands of their fellow Marines. For almost four years, from 1942 to 1945, the code talkers fought in battle after battle. Their unbreakable code helped make sure the enemy could not intercept military communications and that

Marines were protected. The code, created using the Navajo language, was never broken. Then, for almost twenty-five years after the war ended, their story was kept as secret as their code—but now it can be told

CHAPTER 1
The Navajo

For more than one thousand years, Native Americans of the Navajo Nation have been living in the American Southwest. The Navajo, who call themselves Diné (say: DEE-nay), built homes and villages, created systems of traditions and beliefs, and spoke a unique language.

Europeans arrived on the East Coast of North America in the 1500s and started moving westward toward the lands of the Navajo and many other Native American nations. Soldiers from Spain came to the land of the Navajo in the 1540s. They forced the Navajo off the best farming land and tried to convert the Native Americans to the Spaniards' Catholic religion.

For hundreds of years, the two groups fought throughout the American Southwest, with many deaths on both sides.

In the 1830s, white American settlers began to arrive. A US Army fort was built near Window Rock in 1851, deep in the heart of Navajo territory in what is now Arizona. Soldiers again tried to force the Navajo people off their own land and onto reservations, which were areas

set aside for resettling Native Americans. The reservations were often far from the Native Americans' homes and did not have land that was good for farming or had enough water sources. Few reservations provided much area for shelter. The Navajo tried to resist, but the US Army was too powerful. The army killed horses and sheep, burned cornfields, and killed many Navajo.

Fort Defiance, the US Army fort built near Window Rock

Several times, the army forced the Navajo people on a "Long Walk" to a desolate reservation in New Mexico called Bosque Redondo. Hundreds of Navajo died during several of these forced walks, some of which were as long as 450 miles. The Navajo never gave up, however. After resisting the US Army for decades, they signed

a treaty in 1868 that gave the Navajo back their homeland. Today, that land is the Navajo Nation. It surrounds the Four Corners region of the United States, where Utah, Colorado, Arizona, and New Mexico meet. Through it all, the Navajo people kept their faith, their traditions, and their language.

In the years that followed, the Navajo language that the US government tried to stamp out would come to play a big part in helping them. All armies use codes during wartime, and the US military is no different. They need codes that cannot be "broken," or understood, by other armies. A language that was mostly unknown outside the Navajo Nation proved to be perfect.

The US Army had first used Native American languages in World War I, which was fought from 1914 to 1918. Great Britain, France, Russia, and other nations battled Germany and its allies, Austria-Hungary, Bulgaria, and other countries. The United States joined the war in 1917. Incredibly, even though the United States had treated Native Americans miserably for decades, more than twelve thousand Native Americans fought in World War I. At that time, Native Americans were not even citizens of the United

Code talkers during World War I

States! But they still wanted to do their part in the fight.

The US Army hired Choctaw speakers to use radios and to write messages in their native language. Other Native Americans, including

Comanche, Oneida, and Sac and Fox, took part in battles in Europe by sending and receiving messages. Because these languages were specific to each tribal nation, no outsiders knew how to speak or understand them—including the US Army! The Native American speakers were trusted to pass along messages among other men of their own nations. Germany and its allies didn't have soldiers who spoke those languages, so the messages remained secret.

In 1939, World War II began in Europe. As they had in World War I, the Navajo and other Native Americans were ready to fight. The Navajo government said, "We resolve that the Navajo Indians stand ready as they did in 1918, to aid and defend our government and Constitution against all . . . armed conflict."

In early 1942, a man named Philip Johnston read about the use of Native American languages during World War I. Johnston was one of the few non-Navajo people who could speak the Navajo language. He had grown up in the Navajo Nation in Arizona, where his parents were missionaries. Johnston wrote to the US Marines suggesting that the Navajo language could be the basis for an unbreakable code.

Philip Johnston

On February 28, 1942, Johnston arranged a test to show the Marines how the Navajo language might be used as a code. Four Navajo speakers were matched against four Marine messengers. Using radios, the Navajo speakers accurately sent a test message translated from English into Navajo in twenty seconds. The other messengers took half an hour using the code already in use by the Marines. Major General Clayton Vogel ordered Johnston to find Navajo men to train for this new mission.

World War II

In 1939, German armed forces invaded Poland. England and France joined with other European countries to fight against Germany's advances. At the same time in the Pacific, the empire of Japan began its own invasive attacks on nearby countries and islands.

On December 7, 1941, Japanese planes flew across the Pacific Ocean and bombed US Navy ships at Pearl Harbor, Hawaii. The next day, the United States and Japan were at war. The United States soon joined the war in Europe against Germany as well.

More than forty countries made up the Allies that fought Germany, Italy, and Japan. Battles took place across Europe, in North Africa and in Asia, and on many Pacific islands.

Together, all these conflicts were called World War II.

The Allies won the war when Germany surrendered on May 7, 1945, following the death of its leader, Adolf Hitler. Japan surrendered on September 2, after the United States dropped two deadly atomic bombs on two of Japan's major cities.

Attack on Pearl Harbor

CHAPTER 2
Marine Boot Camp

In April 1942, Philip Johnston returned to the Navajo lands where he had once lived. Because of a lack of support from the US government, life there had become very difficult. The American states that controlled the Navajo lands did not provide enough electricity or telephone lines for the Navajo. And they did a poor job running the school systems there. When Johnston called for volunteers, more than two hundred Navajo men showed up. Joining the Marines looked like an opportunity to improve their situation. It was a good job. Being a Marine could also be dangerous work, but the Navajo men believed they came from a long line of warriors, and they were ready to fight.

Jesse Smith

Samuel "Jesse" Smith remembered that "old men with bows and arrows came to the trading post and wanted to go to war and fight the [Japanese] and save their land. I had the same idea. I wanted to save our land." Without telling them what their job would be, Johnston chose twenty-nine men who spoke both English and Navajo well.

One of the young Navajo volunteers like Jesse was Chester Nez. He had grown up tending sheep with his family. In 1934, he had been sent away to a junior high school at Fort Defiance, Arizona, which had once actually been Navajo land. At the school, the teachers tried to train the Navajo not to speak their native language or to follow their customs. They forced them to speak only English. At the school, Chester first learned his birthday was in January 1921. Before that, he had kept track of time by the seasons, not by months and years. He later went to high school in Tuba City, Arizona. He continued to learn English but always spoke Navajo at home.

Chester Nez

Chester had heard about the Pearl Harbor attack in school. He later wrote, "We . . . had been born to the warrior tradition. Like other Navajos, we saw ourselves as inseparable from the earth we lived upon. And as protectors of what is sacred, we were . . . eager to defend our land."

When he was twenty-one years old, Chester was accepted as a Marine recruit. His roommate at school, Roy Begay, was also part of the original group. Carl Gorman was thirty-five, and that was too old to join. So he changed his age to thirty so he could get in. Dean Wilson was too young to join. In the Marines' recruiting office, he saw his file on a desk. He slipped out a paper that showed that his parents had not given their permission and threw it away. "That's how I got in at age sixteen," he remembered.

Wilsie Bitsie was just barely tall enough to qualify for the Marines. Eugene Crawford, William McCabe, and Harry Tsosie were among the total of twenty-nine Navajo men who were chosen. They got on a bus for a long ride to San Diego, California, where they would go through training called "boot camp" at Marine Corps Base Camp Pendleton.

Twenty-nine Navajo men prepare to head
to Camp Pendleton for training.

After Chester got to the camp, he was given uniforms and weapons. He was shown the bunkhouses where he and the other Navajo Marines would sleep. And he met their trainers, called drill instructors.

At about five o'clock the next morning, the drill instructors woke up Chester and the other

Navajo—loudly! They burst into the bunk room, yelling and shouting instructions. Chester was very surprised. Navajo people rarely raised their voices. They spoke softly to one another. Life for the twenty-nine Navajo at Camp Pendleton would be very different from life in the Navajo Nation.

The Marines kept Chester and the other men to a very tight schedule. Every minute of the day was packed with work, training, or meals. The Navajo were not used to this, and it took a while to adjust. Also, in the Navajo culture, it is not polite to look someone in the eyes. In the Marines, it's a requirement. "Look me in the eye, Marine," the drill instructor screamed at Chester. He had to adjust to his new life quickly.

It helped that doing hard work was nothing new. Most of the Navajo had worked all their lives, often outside. They also enjoyed the plentiful food in the Marine camp. Chester's favorite was a canned meat called Spam, and he also liked Vienna sausages.

The Navajo also proved to be excellent marksmen. Chester had used guns for hunting and protecting his sheep. The all-Navajo Platoon 382 earned one of the camp's best scores in pistol and rifle shooting at targets.

The Marine trainers were trying to make sure the Navajo, and all the Marines, were tough and ready to deal with any problems that came up in war. One night, pairs of Marines were sent out to stay in the desert. They were given just one canteen of water. Chester, Carl, and the other Navajo drank the water, and then refilled the canteens with liquid from cactus plants.

They had learned how to find this water in the
desert on Navajo lands. The other Marines came
back with empty canteens! Also, the long miles

of marching and running were no problem for the Navajo Marines. They often traveled long distances on foot in the wide-open Navajo Nation.

The Navajo were not perfect. For missing assignments or for not completing a job, they were given demerits and light punishment. Wilsie earned more than the others. For forgetting his rifle one time, he had to stand outside with a bucket on his head. For being late too often, he had to bathe Sergeant Duffy, a bulldog that was a mascot for Camp Pendleton.

The men also found time for a little fun. When the Navajo Marines were marching, they often chanted in their native language. The drill instructors thought the Navajo were counting their steps as they marched. Instead, the Navajo Marines were making jokes about the instructors!

After ten weeks, the Navajo men had become Marines. One of their training commanders wrote to the group, "Yours has been one of the outstanding platoons in the history of this Recruit Depot. . . . You obey orders like seasoned and disciplined soldiers. You have maintained rugged health. . . . The Marine Corps is proud to have you in its ranks."

A few days later, on June 29, all the Navajo Marines were sent to nearby Camp Elliott. They were taken to a room and told they were going to get a special mission. Eugene Crawford remembered thinking that if this boring room was their new home, that the mission probably wasn't anything special.

But then the group was told that their new assignment in the Marines would be something very secret, and something very special indeed.

CHAPTER 3
The Secret Language of War

Why did the Marines need the Navajo men to create a secret code? A big reason was that most of the codes that the United States was using had already been broken by Japan's military. Codes are supposed to be secret. "Broken" meant that Japan had figured out the US code and could read it as easily as the US forces could. The situation had to change to protect America's soldiers against the Japanese military.

Success in war often means surprising the enemy. Each side makes plans that they don't want the other side to know about. They need to know where to send troops or supplies. Or they need to tell their fellow soldiers where to meet them for a battle. If their enemy learns that information, then they can cause great damage. For example, if an army sends a message in code to have one hundred soldiers meet on Hill B, they will need to keep that location secret. If their enemy can read that message, they will then send two hundred or three hundred soldiers to Hill B and win the battle.

So how do armies send messages and information without revealing their secrets to one another? For thousands of years, the answer was to use secret writing called codes and ciphers. These are ways of sending information that can only be understood by someone who also knows how to read them.

A cipher (say: SY-fer) changes each letter to another letter or symbol. A code changes whole words and phrases instead of individual letters.

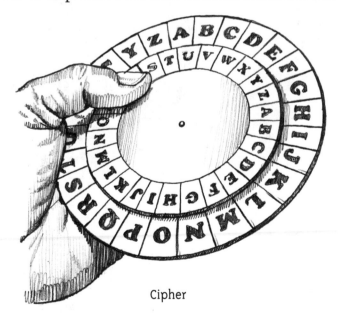

Cipher

A code can also swap words for other words. Both the sender and receiver have to know what each code word means. For instance, if a radioman called out "Rabbit fox mountain star," that would mean nothing to most listeners. But if the receiver knew that those words were code for "Start the attack now!" then the message would be understood.

The Marines told the new Navajo Marines that it was their job to come up with a way to use Navajo words to create an unbreakable code.

Chester, Carl, Wilsie, and the others finished listening to instructions from a Marine officer. He told them that they needed a Navajo word to stand for each letter of the English alphabet. Then he gave them a list of military words, such as *tank*, *airplane*, *general*, and *camp*. The list included more than two hundred terms. The Navajo men were told to come up with Navajo words as code for each of the words on the list.

The officer also said that everything they were doing was top secret. They could tell no one about their mission or their work.

Then he left and locked the door behind him.

CHAPTER 4
Creating the Navajo Code

For a few minutes in that room at Camp Elliott, the Navajo Marines just looked at one another. In the Marines, they had learned to march, fire rifles, put up tents, and follow orders. But this was very different. They were surprised that anyone wanted them to speak Navajo.

"When I went to school, they told me not to speak my own language," code talker Samuel Tso said later. "When I did speak my own language, they used to punish me. Thirteen years later, they asked me to use my language. [I thought,] 'You told me to forget it, how come you want it?' That's the time they started saying, 'Please, we need you. We need you for your language.'"

Wilsie said that he was a pretty good typist, so

he got ready to work. He suggested that they start with the alphabet. Then, one of their first tasks was to make sure to choose words that sounded different so they would not be confused.

Chester remembered later that the group worked very well together. "The ability to live in unity, learned on the reservation . . . proved invaluable to our [new] assignment."

The men chose words that were familiar and easy to remember. For the English letter *A*, they used the Navajo word for ant, *wol-la-chee*. *B* was

Weasel

for bear, or *shush*. Many of the letters stood for animals they all knew from their life back home, such as goat, horse, lamb, sheep, and weasel.

The men were taken back to the room day after day. They built the entire alphabet. Then they started connecting Navajo words to military terms. Spelling out every word would take too much time, so code words were used for terms they would say often.

A fighter plane was called *da-he-tih-hi*, which

means hummingbird. A battleship was called a *lotso*, or whale. They made code words for military ranks, for countries, and for months of the year. They came up with more than two hundred code words, such as for *hospital*, *order*, *river*, *troops*, and *signal*.

"There were days that I thought my head would burst," remembered Crawford. "Sometimes we would spend three or four hours on just one word!"

For other words that were not on the list, the men used the alphabet code. The word *eggs* was spelled out *"dzeh-klizzie-klizzie-dibeh."* Those words meant "elk-goat-goat-sheep," or *E-G-G-S.*

"dzeh-klizzie-klizzie-dibeh"

The Navajo Marines spent many hours memorizing the long list of words until they knew them perfectly. As they made the code, they found they had an advantage. There is no written Navajo language. It is only spoken and heard. So memorizing a new list of words was nothing new for these men.

"In Navajo, everything is in the memory—songs, prayers, everything. That's the way we were raised," remembered William McCabe.

Working in teams of two, the men practiced using radios. One man listened to what was said on the radio and repeated it. The other translated the message in his head and then wrote it down in English. One day during their training, Wilsie and some others were taken by military police to meet with a Marine general. He wanted Wilsie to listen to a mysterious tape recording that had been made. The general was so worried about the sounds

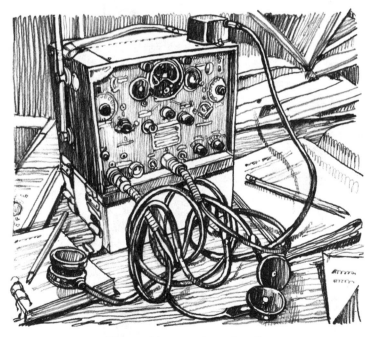

Radio used by Navajo code talkers

on the tape that he had put the whole base on alert for an enemy attack. He thought the recording meant that the Japanese were coming. But it was a recording of the Navajo code talkers practicing!

The code was such a big secret that even that general had not been told about it. From then on, other parts of Camp Elliott were alerted when the Navajo were practicing.

In October 1942, twenty-seven of the original twenty-nine Navajo were sent west toward the fighting on islands in the Pacific Ocean. Some men stayed behind in Camp Elliott to train new Navajo recruits. Dozens more Navajo volunteers were on the way to become Marines and to learn the code. The Marines had seen what the first code talkers could do. They wanted to get more Navajo code talkers ready to join them.

The Navajo Letter Code

This is the first alphabet that was created in the Navajo code. Later, other code words were added for letters that were used often. How would you spell your name using the Navajo code alphabet?

Letter of the Alphabet	Navajo Word	English Word
A	wol-la-chee	ant
B	shush	bear
C	moasi	cat
D	be	deer
E	dzeh	elk
F	ma-e	fox
G	klizzie	goat
H	lin	horse
I	tkin	ice
J	tkele-cho-gi	jackass*

K	klizzie-yazzie	kid
L	dibeh-yazzie	lamb
M	na-as-tso-si	mouse
N	nesh-chee	nut
O	ne-ahs-jah	owl
P	bi-so-dih	pig
Q	ca-yeilth	quiver
R	gah	rabbit
S	dibeh	sheep
T	than-zie	turkey
U	no-da-ih	Ute**
V	a-keh-di-glini	victor
W	gloe-ih	weasel
X	al-an-as-dzoh	cross (an X)
Y	tsah-as-zih	yucca
Z	besh-do-gliz	zinc

*Jackass is a male donkey.
**Ute is the name of another Native American nation.

CHAPTER 5
The Code in Action

The key to the Navajo code was secrecy. The Japanese could never find out about it. The men in the Navajo platoon were forbidden from writing home about it. They could not talk to other Marines about the code, either. Their mission was kept secret even from many of the Marine officers they met. All that secrecy meant that getting the Navajo code into action would take a little extra work.

First, they faced a long sea voyage. Chester, Wilsie, and eight other code talkers traveled aboard the USS *Lurline*. Other code talkers headed west on different ships; the Marines did not want to risk them all on a single transport. On the *Lurline*, most of the Navajo were seasick for days.

USS *Lurline*

Life in the Arizona desert had not prepared them
for the big waves of the Pacific Ocean. The ship
stopped first in Hawaii, but the code talkers were
not allowed to go ashore there. Their mission had
to remain a secret. The next stop, more than two
weeks later, would be the island of New Caledonia,
about nine hundred miles east of Australia.

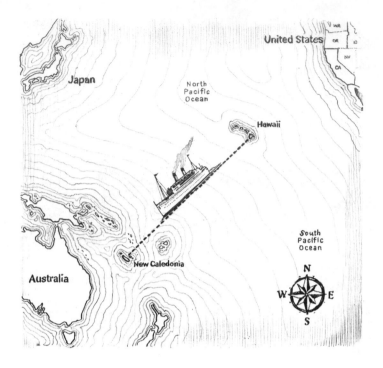

There, all the Marines continued training. The code talkers practiced their code as well as hand-to-hand combat drills. They learned how to land on a beach from small boats. They also tried to adjust to the weather. South Pacific islands are hot and very humid. Often, the men would jump into the ocean in full uniform just to cool off for a few moments.

US Marines landing on Guadalcanal

Then, in early November 1942, the code talkers got their orders. They would join the First Marine Division heading to Guadalcanal, part of the Solomon Islands north of New Caledonia. The US military had recently landed on Guadalcanal, but most of the island was still held by the Japanese. This was one of the first stops in the United States' island-hopping strategy.

Island Hopping

Before US forces could attack Japan itself, they had to take back a series of islands held by the Japanese Army. The plan was for the US forces to move west from place to place, "island hopping," as it was called. With each successful mission on an island, they would get closer to Japan itself. Using Navy ships and airplanes and Marine landing forces, the US military aimed for places like the Marshall Islands, the Solomon Islands, the Mariana Islands, Iwo Jima, and others.

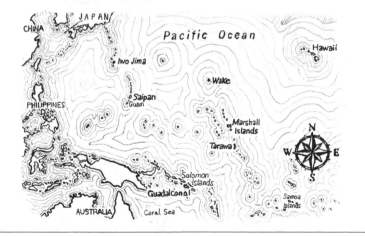

After a short journey on a smaller ship, the code talkers waded through the surf to the beach at Guadalcanal. All around them, they could see the signs of a recent battle. Smoking holes dotted the sand. Broken and blasted equipment littered the beach. Navajo Marine William McCabe

remembered the men looking for the place where they were supposed to report for duty. On the way there, they had to dive for cover when a Japanese fighter plane flew over and fired machine-gun bullets at them!

After locating the Marines' headquarters,

the code talkers faced another challenge: the officer in charge of codes didn't think the code talkers could beat the system he was using! He gave them a message that he boasted his system could send and receive in less than four hours. McCabe told the officer he would just need two minutes. When McCabe handed the officer the response a couple of minutes later, the officer was shocked. "That was the end of the test," McCabe said later. "The code talkers made a believer of [him]."

Within hours, Chester, Roy, and the others were in the thick of the action. One of their first messages directed artillery fire on an enemy position. *"Al-deel-tahi,"* they sent, which meant "destroy." A moment later, loud explosions showed that their directions had been perfect. For the next two days, almost without sleep, they sent message after message: Send ammunition here. Aim more artillery there. Move this platoon to another area.

And on and on. They got a few minutes of sleep when they could, but the noise of the bombs and guns going off all around them made it difficult.

The Navajo were saving the lives of their fellow Marines with their coded messages by directing artillery fire (large, heavy guns and tanks) and helping to position troops.

Artillery

The Navajo code talkers had more than proven their worth on Guadalcanal. But the war continued, and other dangerous challenges awaited them, including their most important mission yet.

CHAPTER 6
Code-Talker Life

As the island-hopping campaign of World War II continued throughout 1943 and 1944, Navajo code talkers joined their fellow Marines, landing in places such as Guam, Iwo Jima, Bougainville, New Britain, and Peleliu.

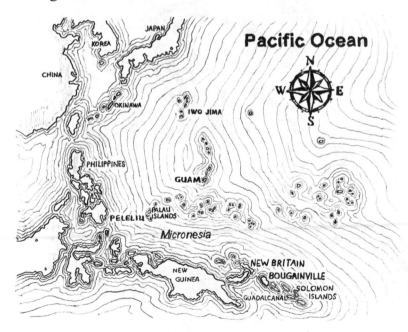

Meanwhile, newly trained Navajo code talkers were arriving from Camp Elliott to join the original group. After Guadalcanal, Marine Major General Alexander Vandegrift sent a message to Camp Elliott. "This Navajo code is terrific," he wrote. "The enemy never understood it. We don't understand it either, but it works. Send us some more Navajos." By the end of the war, more than four hundred Navajo served as code talkers!

Major General
Alexander Vandegrift

As the number of code talkers and their missions grew, so did the code itself. More and  more military terms were added. For example, a grenade is a small, handheld explosive. The Navajo called grenades *ni-ma-si*, which means potatoes. The word for a fort became *ah-na-sozi*, which means cliff dwelling. A tank's code word was *chay-da-gahi*, a tortoise.

New Navajo words for English letters were added to confuse the Japanese Army, too. A key way to break a code is to look at how often letters are repeated. *E*, *A*, and *S*, for example, are among the most-used English letters. So if a code breaker sees the same cipher used often, there's a good chance it might be *E*, *A*, or *S*. To help prevent that, about a dozen often-used English letters were given Navajo alternates. The letter *A* could be *wol-la-chee* (ant), *be-la-sana* (apple), or *tse-nill* (ax).

Though the code talkers' day-to-day work was about maintaining communications, life in the battle zones was still dangerous. To reach places where it would be safe to speak on their radios, they often had to avoid machine-gun fire or enemy artillery. The code talkers spent many

scary nights huddled in trenches or foxholes as
bullets zinged above them.

The Japanese tried their best to stop the code talkers from doing their job. The Japanese radiomen could hear all the words that the Navajo were sending; they just couldn't understand them. Still, to try to distract the Marines from their coding work, the Japanese soldiers blasted loud noises or banged pots and pans into the radio broadcasts.

Sometimes the danger was not from the Japanese forces. Most Marines did not know who the code talkers were or how important their mission was. And some soldiers thought that the dark-skinned Navajo men looked Japanese.

Eugene Crawford

Eugene Crawford was once threatened with a pistol by another Marine who thought Crawford was sneaking into camp. The Marine did not let Crawford go until an officer told him the real story. Several other code talkers also told stories about being mistaken for Japanese soldiers.

The code talkers worried what would happen if they were caught. Would the Japanese torture them to reveal the Navajo code? Because of fears of mistaken identity and capture, many Navajo code talkers were given Marine bodyguards. These Marines traveled everywhere with the code talkers. They made sure the code talkers were not bothered by fellow US soldiers and also protected them from enemy attack. "[Mine] stuck to me like glue. If I went to the [bathroom], so did he," remembered Eugene Crawford.

The code talkers weren't bothered by having bodyguards. And some later said that they didn't even know they had them! But many other aspects of war upset the Navajo more than the other Marines. In the Navajo culture, the bodies of the dead are something to be avoided. Navajo believe that spirits of the dead sometimes stay with the bodies. From the moment they waded ashore on Guadalcanal, Chester and his fellow Navajo saw many dead soldiers, American and Japanese. Dan Akee later said that his fear of corpses "was one of the hardest things to get over" in the war.

Amid all this danger, the Navajo depended on their culture to help them survive. Most had been sent off from home with a song-filled ceremony called the Blessingway, and with prayers from family members. As they did their dangerous work in the Pacific, each code talker also carried his own Navajo medicine bag. Chester's bag had a black arrowhead on a string, a small white rock, and corn pollen from his family's farm. "That medicine bag connected me to home, to the prayers of my relatives," wrote Chester later. "It protected me and gave me confidence that I would survive."

Every morning, the men took a tiny pinch of the pollen and touched the top of their heads and their tongues with it. Then they pointed to each of the four directions to finish their morning blessing.

Letters from home also helped the Navajo stay connected to their families. Some of the Navajo Marines also sent back small bits of their uniforms. This clothing would then be used in ceremonies back home in which relatives asked the gods for protection for their loved ones.

The Marines continued their island-hopping strategy. The United States' military leaders looked at their next target: Iwo Jima (say: EE-woh JEE-mah). Helping to capture this tiny volcanic island would prove to be the code talkers' toughest mission against the Japanese.

Iwo Jima

CHAPTER 7
Iwo Jima

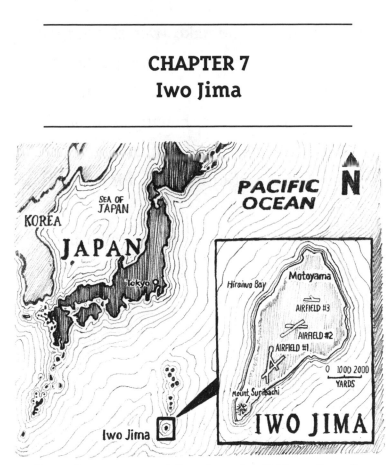

Iwo Jima is an island only 760 miles from Tokyo, the capital city of Japan. Its name means "sulfur island" in Japanese. It was created by an exploding volcano, which continued to spew bad-smelling sulfur gas from inside the earth.

If the Marines could take over this important island, US bomber airplanes would be able to take off and land on the Iwo Jima airfields to easily reach Japan itself. Having control of Iwo Jima might help end the war and save tens of thousands of lives. But the fight for it would not be easy.

The first moves in the battle came from the air. No civilians lived on Iwo Jima, but more than twenty thousand Japanese soldiers had landed there months earlier. In February 1945, US airplanes began bombing the island. The United States hoped that the explosions would make a land attack safer for their own troops. But the Japanese had dug thousands of caves and tunnels, and most were able to hide from the bombardment. They also knew the importance of keeping control of Iwo Jima, and they fought back fiercely.

On February 19, Navajo code talkers were

Cave dug by Japanese soldiers on Iwo Jima

among the six thousand Marines who made
the first landing on Iwo Jima. Because larger
ships could not bring the men into the shallow
waters along the coast of the island, smaller boats
called landing craft were used to get through
the surf. Code talker Merril Sandoval's landing
craft overturned. He was pitched into the water
and lost almost all of his radio equipment.

He said later that he was glad he had taken swimming lessons back at Camp Elliott. As he reached the beach, he saw US planes hit by enemy fire crash into the rocky island.

Once on the island, Samuel Holiday and the others found that the soft black sand was almost impossible to walk in. For every step forward, Samuel slid two steps back. And it smelled like rotten eggs from the sulfur that oozed out of the volcanic ground.

For the first few hours, the Marines slogged through sand and water. Then, suddenly, the Japanese poured out of their tunnels and attacked. Now pinned on the beach, the surprised Marines were hit by machine-gun fire and mortars.

Mortars and mini rocket

Samuel Sandoval said he had to crawl over and around the bodies of Marines. "I saw bullets hitting the sand directly in front of me." So much black sand was blown into the air, remembered Samuel, that "even the sun looked sad."

The fighting was so intense that the code talkers often had to put down their radios and fire

on the enemy. Samuel Holiday was nearly killed by a grenade that rolled out from underneath a dead Japanese soldier. Bill Toledo braved enemy fire to help carry a stretcher with a wounded Marine. The other Marine carrying the stretcher was hit, too, so Bill had to drag both men to safety.

As the fighting continued, the code talkers dug into foxholes—pits in the sand—and got to work.

They relayed message after message, sending help to Marines in trouble. They also directed ships and planes to bomb Japanese positions. They had to do their work even as bullets flew all around them. Most went without sleep. In the first two days of the attack, according to Marine Major Howard Connor, the Navajo code talkers "sent and received over eight hundred messages without an error."

Each day, more Marines arrived. Slowly, they drove the Japanese from the caves and captured more and more of the island. On the fifth day after the landing, the Marines cheered when a US flag was raised on Mount Suribachi, the island's highest point.

Mount Suribachi

Teddy Draper

Navajo code talker Teddy Draper was on the mountain, watching, and he sent out the message about the flag raising on Mount Suribachi. However, it took more than a month after that for the Marines to take full control of the entire island. During the fighting, three code talkers gave their lives: Paul Kinlahcheeny, Sam Morgan, and Willie Notah. Finally, on March 26, 1945, the Marines defeated the last Japanese defenders of Iwo Jima.

The contributions of the Navajo code talkers on Iwo Jima were enormous; without their ability to send vital information in secret, thousands more Marines might have died.

Major Connor wrote later, "Were it not for the Navajos, the Marines would never have taken Iwo Jima."

Raising the Flag on Iwo Jima

One of the most famous and lasting images
of World War II is a photo taken on Iwo Jima on
February 23, 1945. Six Marines are shown raising a
pole with the American flag on Mount Suribachi.
Earlier, a small US flag had been raised there. A few
hours later, more Marines came with the larger flag.
Photographer Joseph Rosenthal watched the men
raise the big flag, and he took the photo of them

as the flag fluttered in the wind. His photo inspired millions of Americans. It was later the model for a statue at the US Marine Corps War Memorial in Arlington National Cemetery in Washington, DC, that honors Marines who gave their lives for their country. One of the six Marines in the photo was Ira Hamilton Hayes, a member of the Pima Nation.

The photo is called *Raising the Flag on Iwo Jima*. The man who took the picture, Joseph Rosenthal, had been rejected as a soldier by the US Army because of his poor eyesight. But he was later named an honorary Marine in recognition of the powerful image he created on Iwo Jima.

Joseph Rosenthal

CHAPTER 8
Going Home

Some of the code talkers were part of yet another Pacific island attack, when they helped capture Okinawa in June 1945. While they rested there in early August, they heard about the atomic

bombs that had been dropped on Japan.

After those terrible attacks, the Japanese empire surrendered. The war was over. On duty on several Pacific islands, the Navajo Marines celebrated when they got the news.

Code talkers Paul Blatchford and Rex Malone were chosen to serve in Japan while United States forces remained in control. Blatchford was given the job of sending all the news and reports about the atomic bombs' destruction back to the United States using the Navajo code.

Atomic Bombs

Throughout World War II, scientists had been working to build very powerful new weapons for the US military. Fueled by the energy of exploding atoms, the bombs would be the most destructive in history. When he was told the bombs were ready, US president Harry Truman decided to use them in an effort to end the war quickly.

On August 6, 1945, the first atomic bomb was dropped on Hiroshima, Japan. More than sixty thousand people were killed and sixty-nine thousand injured, some with terrible burns from radiation from the blast. On August 9, a second bomb was dropped on Nagasaki, killing nearly forty thousand more people. The cities' destruction forced the Japanese government to surrender and end the war.

Atomic cloud rising over Nagasaki, Japan

Even after the war, the code talkers were told to keep their secret. They could not tell family or friends what they had done, only that they had served in the Marines. The hope was to keep the code secret in case they were ever needed again.

"We were told just to say we were in the war. That was all right. We weren't looking for glory," remembered code talker Samuel Billison.

Recovering from the horrible circumstances of war is difficult. Like many soldiers, some of the code talkers struggled. George Kirk had nightmares about Japanese soldiers attacking him in the night. He worked with a Navajo medicine man to help his dreams go away. Roy Notah did the same after dreaming of Japanese dragons.

Roy Notah visiting a Navajo medicine man

Chester Nez had completed his duty before Iwo Jima, but he spent time in a hospital recovering from his experiences. He, too, had "horrifying dreams of unearthly battles." When he finally made it back to New Mexico in October, a federal official giving him a new ID card said, "You're not a full citizen of the United States, you know." Even after risking his life in war, he and his fellow Navajo were still discriminated against in the United States. In fact, Native Americans were not allowed to vote in every state until 1962!

At home, Chester's father welcomed him. "I am relieved to have you home safely, my son. My daily prayers have been answered." But Chester also wrote that there was no special celebration for him. "We Navajos don't celebrate the accomplishments of one who has done his expected duty," he wrote, "so although the homecoming was joyous, there was no reason to celebrate my bravery." Chester later went to the University of Kansas and worked for the Veterans Administration.

Samuel Holiday returned to the United States in late 1945 as well. While traveling home to Arizona, he was not allowed to eat at a café because it was for "white people only." Once he was home, his family helped him recover from the war with an Enemy Way ceremony.

To drive away the spirits of the enemy, the Navajo sang, chanted, and prayed together. They created a sand painting that symbolized the enemy. Then the sand was wiped away. Many code talkers went through these ceremonies to help them heal from the effects of the war.

Samuel later became a Navajo police officer and a park ranger, and he worked in mining. He also learned to perform Navajo ceremonies for his people.

There were some men, including Navajo code talkers, who never healed or recovered from  the stress of the war. They were not alone. Ira Hayes, a member of the Pima Nation, died from his dependence on alcohol ten years after returning home from the war. He was only thirty-two years old.

Ira Hayes

Most other Navajo code talkers went on with their lives, their brave work in the war a secret from everyone except one another. Carl Gorman became an artist. Teddy Draper taught thousands of young people the Navajo language. Harold Foster had a long career with the Bureau of Indian Affairs Health Service (now known as the Indian Health Service). Dean Wilson was one of several Navajo who stayed in the Marines for many years after the war, though they no longer served as code talkers.

Carl Gorman

While the Marines appreciated what the Navajo had done, the feeling was mutual. "The Marines gave me confidence that I could do what was asked of me and succeed," said Harold Foster. All the code talkers were very proud of their service.

Harold Foster, 1976

CHAPTER 9
Delayed Honors

In 1968, the United States government finally revealed the secret of the Navajo code talkers. The Marines had decided that they would never need the code again, so the story could be told. In Chicago the following summer, a reunion of Marines honored the code talkers in public for the first time. Two years later, a gathering of dozens of Marine code talkers was held at Window Rock in Arizona. They were able to share their stories with their friends and families, who began to understand just how important their fathers, sons, and brothers had been. The families heard about the dangers they had faced and learned about the lives they had saved.

At that event, the men formed the Navajo Code Talkers Association. Its mission is to spread the word of the code talkers' bravery to inspire young Navajo and other people. The association created a special uniform for its members. A gold shirt is for the corn pollen they carried. A red cap is for the Marines. Tan pants represent the earth they come from.

Navajo Code Talkers Association uniform

The work of the association has helped to greatly expand the number of young Navajo studying their own language.

As the story of the code talkers spread, more honors were bestowed on them. In 1982, the United States Congress honored the code talkers, too. President Ronald Reagan named August 14 National Navajo Code Talkers Day.

In 1999, the toy maker Hasbro created a G.I. Joe action figure in honor of the code talkers. The Navajo Code Talker G.I. Joe spoke seven of the Navajo code phrases (and their English translations), including "Suribachi secured."

In 2001, the original twenty-nine code talkers were honored with gold Congressional Medals. All the other code talkers received silver medals. President George W. Bush spoke at a ceremony during which the medals were awarded. "We recall a story that all Americans can celebrate. . . .

It is a story of [an] ancient people called to serve in a modern war." Chester Nez proudly saluted as he received his medal. "He's our commander in chief, and you salute your commander in chief. You don't shake his hand," Chester wrote later.

In 2014, Chester was the last of the original twenty-nine Navajo code talkers to pass away. He was ninety-three. He had been part of the Navajo Code Talkers Association from its first days.

Chester Nez in 2014

In 2017, while serving in the Marines on Okinawa, Marine Corps Lance Corporal Jeanette Fernando climbed Mount Suribachi.

Jeanette Fernando, granddaughter
of Navajo Marine Thomas Sandoval

She looked down on the island and remembered the bravery of the code talkers. One was her grandfather, Thomas Sandoval. "I'm able to be in Iwo Jima because of my ancestors, because of

the Marines who fought so proudly before me," she said later.

Thanks to the Navajo Code Talkers Association,

the story of Thomas Sandoval, Chester Nez, Samuel Holiday, and the others will never be forgotten. "Our story is not one of sorrow, like the Long Walk," wrote Chester, ". . . but one of triumph."

Timeline of the Navajo Code Talkers

1917–1918 — Native Americans first serve in the US military during World War I and use their nations' languages as codes

1941 — The United States enters World War II after Japanese forces attack Pearl Harbor in Hawaii

1942 — April: Philip Johnston helps recruit the first twenty-nine Navajo code talkers to the Marine Corps

— June: The Navajo Marines create the first version of the Navajo code

— Navajo code talkers go into action for the first time, when they participate in the Battle of Guadalcanal

1943–1944 — Navajo code talkers join fellow Marines in attacks on Guam, Peleliu, and other islands in the Pacific

1945 — February 19–March 26: Navajo code talkers take part in the capture of Iwo Jima

— September 2: World War II ends when Japan surrenders

1968 — Secret of the Navajo code talkers officially revealed by the US government

1971 — Navajo Code Talkers Association is formed

1982 — Navajo code talkers honored by US Congress

2014 — Chester Nez, the last of the original twenty-nine Navajo code talkers, passes away at the age of ninety-three

Timeline of the World

1918 — World War I ends

1927 — The movie *Wings*, about World War I, is released. Two years later, the film wins the very first Academy Award for Best Picture

1929 — Stock exchange crash in the United States marks the beginning of a worldwide Great Depression

1937 — Famed aviator Amelia Earhart disappears during her attempt at an around-the-world flight

1947 — India becomes an independent nation

1956 — Singer Elvis Presley has his first number-one hit with "Heartbreak Hotel"

1960 — A US Navy submersible becomes the first craft to reach the deepest known point in the ocean, 35,800 feet in the Mariana Trench

1962 — Utah becomes the fiftieth state to allow Native Americans to vote

1973 — Native American activists occupy Wounded Knee, South Dakota, to protest discrimination

2008 — Barack Obama is elected the first Black president of the United States

2014 — After a ten-year journey, the robot probe *Philae* becomes the first spacecraft to land on a comet

Bibliography

*Books for young readers

*Aaseng, Nathan. *Navajo Code Talkers: America's Secret Weapon in World War II*. New York: Bloomsbury Children's Books, 1992.

Colburn, George A., dir. *Journey of Remembrance: Navajo Code Talkers*. 2017; Worcester, PA: Dreamscape, 2018. DVD.

*Durrett, Deanne. *Unsung Heroes of World War II: The Story of the Navajo Code Talkers*. Lincoln: University of Nebraska Press, 2009.

Holiday, Samuel, and Robert S. McPherson. *Under the Eagle*. Norman: University of Oklahoma Press, 2013.

McClain, Sally. *Navajo Weapon: The Navajo Code Talkers*. Tucson, AZ: Rio Nuevo Publishers, 2001 (reprint edition).

Nez, Chester, with Judith Schiess Avila. *Code Talker*. New York: Berkeley Caliber, 2011.